Bad Cat, Jess

Written by
Jill Atkins

Illustrated by
Irene Silvino

Vikram is upset.

His pet cat Jess is not on the mat.
Jess is six.

Is Jess in the box?

No, Jess is not in the box.

Is Jess in his bed?

No, Jess is not in his bed.

Did Jess visit the vet?

No, Jess did not visit the vet.
Jess is not ill.

Vikram is sad.

Vikram cannot hug Jess.

I miss Jess.

Will visits Vikram.

"Is the cat big?"

Vikram nods.

Is it a fat cat? Is it as big as a fox?

It **is** a fat cat. It is a bit big.

But Jess is not as big as me!

Will tells Vikram.

"Ha! Let us go and get Jess. Jess is a bad cat, I can tell."

Vikram jogs up to Jess.

"No, Jess, no!"

Vikram picks up Jess.

"Bad cat, Jess!"